TORTOISES

LIVING WILD

Published by Creative Education
P.O. Box 227, Mankato, Minnesota 56002
Creative Education is an imprint of The Creative Company
www.thecreativecompany.us

Design and production by Mary Herrmann
Art direction by Rita Marshall
Printed in the United States of America

Photographs by Alamy (All Canada Photos, blickwinkel, Everett Collection Inc., INTERFOTO, Juniors Bildarchiv, Craig Lovell/Eagle Visions Photography), Corbis (Stapleton Collection), Dreamstime (Pierre-yves Babelon, Mikhail Blajenov, Landd09, lorboaz, Jesús Eloy Ramos Lara, Teddykebab, Xunbin Pan, Joanne Zh), Getty Images (Fotosearch, Gallo Images-Anthony Bannister, Pete Oxford, Kevin Schafer, Paul Souders, Jerry Young, ZSSD), iStockphoto (Rainer von Brandis, Dewitt, Darren Gidney, Darrin Henry, Holly Kuchera, Chet Mitchell, Stacey Newman, photoBlueIce, DARLA Smedley, Nico Smit, Angelika Stern, Alexey Stiop), Photolibrary (Bios/Peter Arnold), Shutterstock (born2bark, clickit, pinggr, Tom Willard), zbynê-k springer, Wikipedia (Hans Hillewaert, Claire Houck, Joseph Smit)

Library of Congress Cataloging-in-Publication Data
Gish, Melissa.
Tortoises / by Melissa Gish.
p. cm. — (Living wild)
Includes bibliographical references and index.
Summary: A look at tortoises, including their habitats, physical characteristics such as their domed shells, behaviors, relationships with humans, and protected status in the world today.
ISBN 978-1-60818-170-4
1. Testudinidae—Juvenile literature. I. Title.

QL666.C584G57 2012
597.92'4—dc23   2011035794

CPSIA: 021413 PO1656
9 8 7 6 5 4 3 2

CREATIVE EDUCATION

TORTOISES

Melissa Gish

It is late March, and a cool breeze bends a sparse
patch of dry grass in the clay desert of eastern

Uzbekistan. The soil around a small burrow begins to shift, and a dry, scaly head emerges.

It is late March, and a cool breeze bends a sparse patch of dry grass in the clay desert of eastern Uzbekistan. The soil around a small burrow begins to shift, and a dry, scaly head emerges, its dark eyes blinking slowly. It is a Russian tortoise rising from six months of winter sleep. Instinct and the faint scent of distant rain have driven the tortoise from his burrow. Thick front legs and sharp claws dig into the dense, yellow clay as the tortoise pulls his five-inch (12.7 cm) body from the burrow. He will not eat for a few days, awaiting the rain that will spark a profusion of growth in the desert—mosses, grasses, and woody shrubs such as white salsola and pink flowering salt cedar. Then the tortoise will spend the next three months filling his belly, drinking rainwater, and searching for a mate before returning to his burrow to escape the scorching heat of summer.

WHERE IN THE WORLD THEY LIVE

■ **Gopher Tortoise**
southeastern
United States

■ **Ploughshare Tortoise**
Madagascar

■ **Indian Star Tortoise**
India and Sri Lanka

■ **Radiated Tortoise**
Madagascar

■ **Galápagos Tortoise**
Galápagos Islands

■ **Speckled
Padloper Tortoise**
South Africa

■ **Hinge-back Tortoise**
sub-Saharan Africa

■ **Asian Brown Tortoise**
India, Indonesia,
Bangladesh, Malaysia,
Myanmar, Thailand

The nearly 50 species of tortoise make their homes in warm, dry places around the world and are highly concentrated in Africa, India, and Southeast Asia, with 4 species present in North America and 4 in Europe. Many species are native to island habitats within those regions. The eight species shown here represent some of the most well known.

LIFE IN A HALF SHELL

L ike many other reptiles, such as lizards and crocodiles, tortoises existed on Earth long before many commonly known dinosaurs appeared. Along with their relatives the turtles and terrapins, tortoises are members of the superorder Chelonia, named for Chelone, a Greek fairy who was turned into a tortoise. There are about 50 species of tortoise in the family Testudinidae, and new subspecies are being discovered practically every year. The family name comes from the classical Latin word *testudo*, which is derived from *testa*, meaning "shell." The word "tortoise" comes from the Latin *tortus* and refers to the tortoise's twisted feet.

Tortoises are **solitary** reptiles. Reptiles are ectothermic animals, meaning that their bodies depend on external sources of heat, and their body temperatures change with the environment. Tortoises are most active in the morning and late afternoon, warming their bodies in the sun. At midday, when the sun becomes stronger, they retreat to shady areas or burrows to prevent overheating. They sleep at night. Like most reptiles, tortoises reproduce by laying eggs.

The flat-shelled pancake tortoise rests between rocks and inflates its lungs to expand its shell, making it impossible to dislodge.

The green sea turtle, a tortoise relative, is one of seven species of sea turtle that spends its entire life in the ocean.

Tortoises are closely related to and may sometimes be confused with turtles. While all turtles are **aquatic** or semiaquatic, and all but one species of tortoise lives on land, the main differences between the two reptiles can be found by observing the shell and feet. A tortoise shell has a higher dome compared with the flatter turtle shell, and a tortoise's feet have claws for digging, while a turtle has **webbed** feet for swimming.

A thick, bony shell protects the tortoise's muscled body. The hard top of the shell, called the carapace, is made of bony scales called scutes. The softer plate on the underside is called the plastron. The two parts are held together by pieces of bone known as bridges. Depending on the species, tortoise shells are shaped differently to accommodate the varying neck shapes. The shells of the six species of hinge-back tortoise are bowl-shaped to allow these animals to enclose their head and legs entirely within their shells. Some tortoises, such as the Galápagos tortoise, have long necks that stretch upward. To allow for this movement, these tortoises have shells that curve upward behind the neck.

Inside the tortoise's body, the spine and ribs are fused to the shell. Unlike most other land animals,

Most yellow-footed tortoises have yellow feet; however, some have brown or orange markings instead.

While tortoises are typically solitary, a group—such as these Seychelles giant tortoises—is known as a bale.

tortoises have no moveable muscle in their chests to aid in breathing. They must inhale and exhale by pumping muscles between their front legs. Tortoises have a slow **metabolism**, so they may spend several days digesting a meal. Despite having strong legs, a tortoise's heavy shell requires it to move slowly; the largest tortoises can walk only about half a mile (0.8 km) per hour. Unlike their turtle cousins, most tortoises are not built for swimming and generally avoid going into the water.

One of the oldest-known tortoises, which lived more than 200 million years ago, was the heavily armored *Proganochelys*. This 3.5-foot-long (1 m) creature had spikes on its long neck, which it could not tuck into its shell. It also had spines on its tail, which ended in a club that it used for defense. Like modern tortoises, the land-dwelling *Proganochelys* was toothless and had a beaked mouth suited to tearing up vegetation.

Today, all tortoises have thick, straight legs with front feet that are shaped like shovels to aid in digging and flat back feet that provide stability. Tortoises have five claws on each front foot and four on each back foot. All tortoises use their claws to dig holes and tunnels, and

Fossils of Proganochelys *found in Greenland, Germany, and Thailand show that it lived near fresh bodies of water.*

Adwaita, an Aldabra giant tortoise housed in India, was the world's oldest tortoise at the time of his death in 2006 at age 255.

When the Galápagos tortoise and the speckled padloper appear side by side, the size difference is striking.

female tortoises also use their claws to dig nests into which they can lay their eggs.

Tortoises range in size from the more than 500-pound (227 kg) Galápagos tortoise of the Galápagos Islands to the speckled padloper tortoise of South Africa, which weighs less than 6 ounces (170 g). Many species of tortoise, including the tiny padloper and those found only on the Galápagos Islands, are under threat from **poaching**, habitat loss, and competition with invasive species. Despite years of conservation efforts to protect the Mojave Desert tortoise, this animal remains on the Endangered Species List, and the population of Madagascar's ploughshare tortoises—the world's rarest tortoises—is estimated to be fewer than 400.

Like many **vertebrates** such as birds, fish, and other reptiles, tortoises have a see-through inner eyelid called a nictitating (*NIK-tih-tayt-ing*) membrane that closes over each eye, wiping dust from the eyeball and shielding the sensitive **pupil** from direct sunlight. Tortoises also have a strong sense of smell because of a special area on the roof of the mouth called the Jacobson's organ. This organ allows the tortoise to detect the chemical particles that make up food and moisture in the air as the tortoise breathes.

**Unlike most
tortoises, Africa's
serrated hinge-
back tortoise
is semiaquatic,
living in swamps
and streams
from The Gambia
to Uganda.**

Locating food by sight and smell, tortoises then use their
rigid beak and strong jaws, which are covered with sharp
ridges made of keratin—the same material found in human
fingernails—to slice off mouthfuls of plant matter. A
tortoise's tongue is short and thick, and while it uses its
tongue to push food down its throat, a tortoise cannot stick
its tongue out past its beak to grasp food.

As lumbering, slow-moving animals, tortoises are
not designed to hunt for food; rather, they are browsers
and opportunistic feeders. They feed on grasses, weeds,
flowers, and herbs. If insects, **larvae**, and worms are
uncovered while a tortoise is browsing, these creatures
will be added to the tortoise's diet. A tortoise's activity
level depends on temperature. If it is too hot, a tortoise
must find a shady place or burrow in which to cool off.
If it is too cold, a tortoise will not feed and must find a
sunny place to warm up. Only when its body is the right
temperature will a tortoise be able to digest food.

Tortoises do not hear high-frequency sounds, but
they do hear and respond to low-frequency sounds as
well as vibrations in the ground. They use this sense
of **seismic** perception to detect approaching predators

and immediately respond by protecting themselves in whatever way possible. Despite their lack of speed, tortoises possess a range of unique characteristics that have allowed them to survive and adapt to changing environments over many millennia.

A tortoise tucked firmly inside its shell is safe from many predators, since extracting it is extremely difficult.

Male and female Galápagos tortoises exhibit sexual dimorphism by being distinctly different sizes.

A tortoise's rate of maturity varies by species. Smaller species with life spans of 25 to 50 years—such as the Indian star tortoise, which reaches no more than 15 inches (38 cm) in length—are ready to mate when they are 6 to 12 years old. With a potential longevity of more than 150 years, larger species, such as the 4.5-foot (1.4 m) Aldabra giant tortoises, do not start mating until they reach 25 years of age. Males and females of the same species look similar, except for their size and an indentation present on the plastron, near the tail, of males. In small species, mature females are generally larger than males, but in big species, the reverse is true. For example, male Galápagos tortoises are twice as large as females.

Breeding season for tortoises varies by geographic location but typically occurs during warm weather, soon after the tortoises emerge from **hibernation**. In some cases, males battle each other for the right to breed with available females. They may ram into each other, biting and pushing in attempts to flip the other over. The stronger tortoise will be the victor, leaving the loser on his back, legs flailing. Weakened tortoises may die in this

Gopher tortoises, 1 of only 4 North American tortoise species, dig burrows that are 30 feet (9 m) long and 8 feet (2.4 m) deep.

A galápago is a Spanish hornless saddle with an upturned front, so Galápagos tortoises are nicknamed "saddlebacks."

manner, but stronger ones will simply right themselves and walk away—sometimes with bloodied faces and legs.

Yet for most tortoise species, mating requires only that the female sit patiently as the male climbs onto her shell. Sometimes the male will bite the female's neck or use his claws to hold her still. However, some tortoise species rely on elaborate courtship rituals. The male ploughshare tortoise walks in circles around his selected female, nudging her and nipping at her neck and front legs; this may go on for hours before mating begins. The male Asian brown tortoise will fully extend his neck and keep his face pointed at his potential mate, a behavior called "fixating." He will also bob his head up and down and from side to side. If the female is receptive, she will allow the male to follow her until he is able to climb upon her shell and hold her to the ground.

Because the act of mating does not always guarantee the production of offspring, male tortoises will mate with as many females as possible. Tortoises rarely make sounds except during mating season. The males of most species hiss and grunt, but some, such as the Galápagos tortoise, make long, low groans and loud roaring noises. The Hermann's tortoise makes a high-pitched squeak, and the radiated tortoise makes a sound like a barking dog.

Females of certain species begin building their nests soon after mating concludes, but females of other species may store their fertilized eggs inside their bodies for up to 18 months while looking for a suitable nest site. Nest materials and construction vary, according to the tortoise's habitat. Female Greek and gopher tortoises dig holes in sandy slopes exposed to full sunlight, while Asian brown tortoises build mounds of moist leaf litter beneath trees.

All tortoise nests must be warm. Whether the sun bakes the soil over a nest or decaying **organic** matter creates heat

Emerging from their burrows only briefly at dawn and dusk, desert tortoises spend up to 95 percent of their lives underground.

Inhabiting mountain forests from southern China to Malaysia, the impressed tortoise feeds mostly on mushrooms.

energy, all tortoise nests must reach about 85 °F (29 °C) to **incubate** the eggs. If the temperature is too low, the eggs may fail to hatch, but if the temperature is too high—above 95 °F (35 °C)—the tortoises may suffer shell deformities such as extra scutes, which will interfere with their abilities to maneuver, mate, and protect themselves from predators.

Some tortoises continue the pattern of mating and nesting up to 9 times per season, and the female lays 3 to 30 eggs at a time. She then covers them with soil or vegetation and leaves the area. The eggs are flexible and leathery when laid, but the shells harden over a period of several weeks. The eggs of smaller species incubate for shorter periods of time than those of larger species. Eggs of the five species of padloper incubate for about 100 days, but eggs of the Galápagos tortoise may incubate for more than twice that long. The level of heat in the nest will determine the gender of the offspring. While exact temperatures vary by species, lower temperatures will produce males, and higher temperatures will produce females. And temperatures between certain ranges can produce either female or male offspring.

With the exception of the Asian brown tortoise, female tortoises do not defend their nests. Before they

even hatch, baby tortoises can fall prey to many nest raiders. In some species, as many as 90 percent of the eggs are eaten by predators. Only two to three percent of hatched tortoises survive to adulthood, as they are preyed upon by raccoons, opossums, badgers, ravens, and other clever animals that are able to pull young tortoises out of their shells. Golden eagles have even been known to carry tortoises high into the air and then drop them to crack open their shells.

When it begins developing inside the egg, a baby

A slow digestive system that filters out toxins allows tortoises to eat certain types of poisonous mushrooms.

Tortoise hatchlings emerge from their eggs fully formed, looking like miniature versions of their parents.

During mating, the male red-footed tortoise makes a pattern of sounds in varied pitches that are similar to a chicken's clucking.

tortoise is folded in half, nose to tail. As it grows, it straightens out, and an egg tooth develops on the tip of its snout. This sharp projection enables the hatchling to slice through the egg's leathery interior membrane and break through the shell. The egg tooth wears away soon afterward. The newly hatched tortoises dig their way out of the nest to take their first breaths. Hatchlings are immediately independent. Even the largest tortoise species are only about three inches (7.6 cm) long as hatchlings.

Tortoises can tolerate cold better than extreme heat. In places where winter temperatures fall below 55 °F (13 °C), tortoises will dig burrows to hibernate, remaining motionless for months. On the other hand, if a tortoise gets too hot and is unable to cool off, it will suffer and often die.

Juvenile and adult tortoises may be eaten by coyotes and kit foxes. Surviving predation in the wild, some tortoises can live more than 80 years, but kept safe and well fed in captivity, many species can live more than 150 years. The oldest animal on Earth is Jonathan, a Seychelles giant tortoise that lives on the grounds of the governor's palace on the remote South Atlantic island of St. Helena. As of 2012, Jonathan was thought to be 180 years old.

It typically takes three to five minutes for a tortoise hatchling to fully emerge from its egg.

FROM "BABY TORTOISE"

You know what it is to be born alone,
Baby tortoise!
The first day to heave your feet little by little from the shell,
Not yet awake,
And remain lapsed on earth,
Not quite alive.

A tiny, fragile, half-animate bean.

To open your tiny beak-mouth, that looks as if it would never open,

Like some iron door;
To lift the upper hawk-beak from the lower base
And reach your skinny little neck
And take your first bite at some dim bit of herbage,
Alone, small insect,
Tiny bright-eye,
Slow one.

To take your first solitary bite
And move on your slow, solitary hunt.
Your bright, dark little eye,
Your eye of a dark disturbed night,

Under its slow lid, tiny baby tortoise,
So indomitable.
No one ever heard you complain. . . .

Voiceless little bird,
Resting your head half out of your wimple
In the slow dignity of your eternal pause.
Alone, with no sense of being alone,
And hence six times more solitary;
Fulfilled of the slow passion of pitching through immemorial ages
Your little round house in the midst of chaos.

Over the garden earth,
Small bird,
Over the edge of all things.

Traveller,
With your tail tucked a little on one side
Like a gentleman in a long-skirted coat.

All life carried on your shoulder,
Invincible fore-runner.

by D. H. Lawrence (1885–1930)

THE WEIGHT OF THE WORLD

In cultures the world over, tortoises are symbols of long life and good fortune. They are also associated with the creation of the world. In **Hindu** tradition, the tortoise is believed to be holding up an elephant, which in turn carries the world on its back. Such imagery of tortoises bearing the weight of the world can be found in European literature as well, as in the poem "Baby Tortoise" by Englishman D. H. Lawrence.

In ancient Greek **mythology**, the tortoise symbolizes silence and humility. Chelone was a fairy who was cursed by the king of the gods, Zeus. According to one story, Chelone was invited to attend the wedding of Zeus and Hera, but because she was so vain, she stood in front of the mirror too long and was late for the celebration. As punishment, Zeus flattened Chelone's house over her back and forced her to carry it with her forever—as a humble tortoise. Later on, the tortoise was thought of as being wise and determined. In a fable by Aesop, the legendary Greek storyteller, the tortoise beats the hare in a footrace because the hare is overconfident and takes a nap during the race, allowing the slow-moving but persistent tortoise to pass him.

The carapace of the succulent-eating African tent tortoise features a striking pattern of yellow or orange stripes.

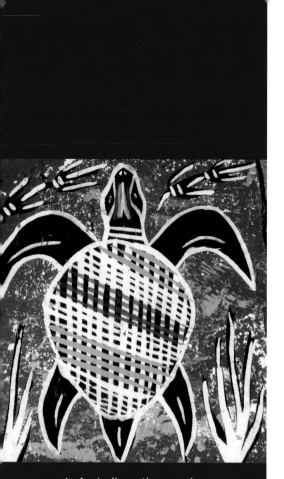

In Australia, native peoples painted a variety of reptiles, including tortoises and sea turtles, on rocks and other surfaces.

The tortoise is mentioned several times in the ancient Egyptian Book of the Dead, a text that was often buried with people for the purpose of guiding them to the afterlife. In the book, which contains the oldest known religious manuscripts in the world, the **mummified** dead are compared to the tortoise—a creature wrapped tightly and securely in its shell. The tortoise spirit Shetu is also called on to help open the sky to allow the dead to leave their coffins.

In Chinese tradition, the tortoise is known as the Black Warrior. It is one of the four major animal spirits, symbolizing the winter season as well as the strength and wisdom of the emperors. For the Chinese, the tortoise also represents long life and harmony. According to the 5,000-year-old herbal remedy document known as the Pen Ts'ao, the tortoise is a symbol of yin and yang, or the balance of opposites. The tortoise's body represents the earth, which is yin, and its shell represents the sky and stars, called the yang. Over thousands of years, the image of the tortoise and its symbolic harmony endured, leading to the emergence of **Tao** (*DOW*) in ancient China.

Similarly, Indian tradition also uses the tortoise to

symbolize balance in the universe. The Hindu story
of Kasyapa, the tortoise god who was the father of all
other **deities** and of humans, teaches that the tortoise is
a sacred animal and must never be captured or harmed.
Nearly 5,000 miles (8,046 km) away, the Yoruba people,
originally from West Africa, include Ijapa, a clever
tortoise, in the folklore of their culture. One tale has Ijapa

*Beihai Park, one of the most
famous landmarks in Beijing,
China, features bronze sculptures
of creatures such as tortoises.*

British artist Arthur Rackham illustrated Aesop's "The Tortoise and the Hare" for a book published in 1912.

dining with a snake, but the snake's deception leaves Ijapa with nothing to eat. To teach the snake a lesson, Ijapa invites him to dinner and tricks him into watching as Ijapa consumes all the food.

In real life, an amazing friendship developed between Owen, a baby hippopotamus stranded on the African coast after a 2004 tsunami, and Mzee, a 130-year-old Aldabra tortoise. After being rescued, Owen was housed with Mzee at Haller Park in Kenya. During their two-year relationship, the hippo and the tortoise—which were roughly the same size at first—ate, slept, and even played together. Owen eventually grew too big for Mzee and was moved to an enclosure with another hippopotamus, but the story of Owen and Mzee's unique bond was captured in a series of books: *Owen and Mzee: The True Story of a Remarkable Friendship* (2006), *Owen & Mzee: The Language of Friendship* (2007), and *Owen & Mzee: Best Friends* (2007). Visitors to their Web site, owenandmzee.com, can read about them and see them in a number of videos.

Perhaps the most well known of the world's tortoises live on the Galápagos Islands, west of the South American country of Ecuador. When 16th-century Spanish

Like any young hippo following its mother, Owen tracked Mzee around their shared enclosure at the park.

During hot weather, many tortoises estivate, or move underground to slow down their metabolism so they can sleep.

explorers traveled to Central and South America in search of gold, they established a shipping route that took them along the coast of Ecuador. In 1535, Spaniard Fray Tomás de Berlanga, the fourth bishop of Panama, discovered the Galápagos Islands—only because his ship drifted there by accident. Finding no food and very little water, Berlanga reported that the distant islands, which are about 605 miles (974 km) from the continent, were worthless, so subsequent explorers largely ignored them.

Pirates, however, found the isolated islands to be perfectly suited to their needs, as they could launch their attacks on gold-carrying ships and then hide from authorities. In 1684, an English pirate named William Ambrosia Cowley mapped the 18 islands and gave them their first English names after his fellow pirates and accomplices. Later, the names would be changed by British naturalist Charles Darwin and again by the government of Ecuador.

The peaceful, slow-moving Galápagos tortoises remained relatively undisturbed during this time, but in the early 1800s, when whale and seal hunters began inhabiting the islands, the tortoises suffered.

The invaders stripped the trees of fruit, and the goats they brought with them ate much of the vegetation. In addition, sailors captured hundreds of thousands of tortoises for their meat. Upon visiting the islands in 1835, Darwin reported that a single ship typically carried away as many as 700 tortoises from the islands. During this period, there were more than 250,000 tortoises on the islands, but by the early 1900s, the population had plummeted to fewer than 10,000. The practice of capturing tortoises continued into the middle of the century, threatening the Galápagos tortoises with **extinction**.

In 1959, Galápagos National Park was established, preserving 97 percent of the islands' land space and protecting their unique wildlife—including the tortoises, whose numbers have been increasing. Once populated by 12 to 15 subspecies of Galápagos tortoise, the Galápagos Islands are now home to about 15,000 individuals in the 10 (or 11) subspecies that still exist. **Ecotourists** who travel to the islands with special permits pay thousands of dollars for the chance to see these tortoises in the wild. The funds help support research and conservation in the Galápagos.

Captain James Colnett of the British Royal Navy created the first accurate sailing chart of the Galápagos in 1798.

The Galápagos hawk, found only on the islands for which it is named, includes tortoise hatchlings in its diet.

TORTOISES IN TROUBLE

The elongated (or yellow) tortoise is one of the most common tortoises found in Asian food markets.

Galápagos tortoises are not the only tortoises facing threats. **Herpetologists** around the world consider the decline of tortoises in Southeast Asia to be a major ecological crisis. These reptiles are under attack from habitat loss, exploitation for food, **commercial** use of their shells, and the pet trade. Because tortoises move slowly, they cannot escape the chainsaws and bulldozers used by loggers, and they are easy targets for people who hunt them or capture their young to sell as pets.

Much research has been conducted in recent years to measure human influence on tortoise populations in Southeast Asia, including a study headed by American biology professor Steven Platt, who traveled to Mount Popa National Park in Myanmar (also known as Burma), a tropical country south of China, in 2010 to study native turtles and tortoises such as the elongated tortoise (also known as the yellow tortoise). Platt's research revealed that, often, when the local people gather mushrooms for food, they discover the tortoises and take them from the park. Because no large tortoises were found in the study, Platt speculated that tortoises are now being captured before

The presence of more than 70,000 humans can make it difficult to preserve natural habitat in the Mapimi Reserve.

Twenty years after the Bolson tortoise was discovered in 1959, Mexico's Mapimi Biosphere Reserve was created to protect its habitat.

they can reach maturity. With fewer mature individuals left to reproduce, elongated tortoise populations are declining in the park, and researchers worry that this could become a trend elsewhere.

Craig Stanford, a professor of anthropology and biology at the University of Southern California, has researched tortoises for more than a decade. His work has taken him to the jungles of Thailand, where, in collaboration with Chulalongkorn University in Bangkok, he undertook the first field study of Asia's largest tortoise, the Asian brown tortoise (also known as the Asian forest tortoise). Weighing 50 to 80 pounds (22.7–36.3 kg), the female of this species is the only tortoise to remain near its nest after egg-laying to defend it from predators. Little else is known about this tortoise, which is a common food source in Thailand. Tracking tortoises and monitoring their burrows, Stanford collects a variety of data, from the tortoise's diet to its travel and reproduction patterns. One fact has already emerged from the study: these rare tortoises are being negatively affected by hunting and are in danger of disappearing from their native habitat.

The pet trade also threatens tortoise populations

around the world. The 2010 discovery of tortoise bones beside the remains of dogs and cats in Stafford Castle in west-central England strongly reinforced existing evidence that tortoises have been kept as pets in Europe since the early 19th century, when wealthy families built collections of exotic animals, called menageries, on their estates. Today, tortoises have become popular pets in many countries because of their perceived ease of care. However, tortoises are actually difficult to keep in captivity, and most perish in the hands of amateurs.

Since tortoises are reptiles, they require adequate exposure to sunshine but should not be allowed to overheat. They are naturally burrowing animals and need an enclosure that prevents them from digging their way out. Also, tortoises have specific dietary requirements that vary by species. Perhaps most importantly, though, the summer estivation and winter hibernation periods of many species necessitate that specific temperatures and humidity levels be met. Many inexperienced pet owners lose their tortoises to illness or disease, or they choose to give up their tortoises when caring for the animals proves to be more work than originally anticipated.

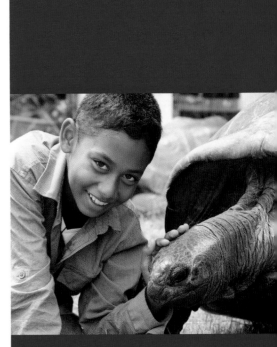

Visitors to St. Helena can meet Jonathan as well as his Aldabra giant tortoise friends: David, Emma, Frederika, and Myrtle.

The spider tortoise, found only on the island of Madagascar, gets its name from the pattern on its shell that resembles a spiderweb.

In 2009, the San Diego Zoo's Institute for Conservation Research partnered with several other organizations to create a rescue and rehabilitation facility for abandoned pet tortoises. While populations of **captive-reared** tortoises are on the rise, the wild populations of various North American desert tortoise species have been declining. Releasing former pets into a protected desert habitat in Nevada is one of the institute's methods of gathering data that could help wild populations.

First, each tortoise's shell is fitted with a radio transmitter. This tiny device sends out a signal that allows researchers to track the tortoise's movements and activities. The transmitter's battery lasts two years. Researchers use the data gathered to determine the best locations for future releases of tortoises. Ultimately, the institute hopes to increase wild populations and save desert tortoises from an uncertain future.

The critically endangered Burmese star tortoise has been the subject of urgent research, as only a few hundred individuals are believed to exist in two protected areas of central Myanmar. These brilliantly colored tortoises suffer extensive poaching due to increased demand in the food

The Burmese star tortoise is found
in dry, deciduous forests where
trees shed their leaves annually.

and pet industries. The Chinese consider tortoise meat a delicacy, and the animals' organs and shells are used in many traditional Asian medicines. In addition, American collectors have been known to pay as much as $7,000 for a live Burmese star tortoise.

The Taipei Zoo in Taiwan, in partnership with California's Turtle Conservancy & Behler Chelonian Center, is involved in the captive-rearing of the Burmese star tortoise. The groups hope to improve breeding techniques, exchange **genetic** material to increase the number of breeding pairs, and promote conservation efforts in the tortoise's native Myanmar. The Turtle Conservancy studies and breeds other species of tortoise as well, including radiated, flat-tailed, and spider tortoises,

Despite many breeding attempts since his capture in 1972, Lonesome George never produced any offspring.

along with two subspecies of Galápagos tortoise.

While only 10 subspecies of Galápagos tortoise still exist, scientists are confident they can revive an 11th species using genetic research and selective breeding. Hunted to extinction by 19th-century sailors, *Chelonoidis elephantopus* exists today only as bones in a museum. As of 2011, Yale University evolutionary biologist Adalgisa Caccone continued using genetic information from the bones to orchestrate a revival of this species by manipulating similar genetic material in some of this tortoise's living relatives. Another subspecies, *Geochelone nigra abingdoni*, may never be revived. Estimated to be about 100 years old, a tortoise named Lonesome George was the last of his kind on Earth. Scientists studied George's genes but were unable to save his subspecies before his death in June 2012.

Despite continued efforts to protect tortoises from logging and poaching, these reptiles face a rocky future. In many wild areas, tortoises exist in stable populations, but in places where these animals must coexist with humans, their numbers are often shockingly low. Without people's conscious efforts to conserve tortoise habitats and food sources, these ancient animals could face their last days on Earth all too soon.

Lonesome George, the last of the Pinta Island giant tortoises, was housed at the Charles Darwin Research Station on Santa Cruz Island.

ANIMAL TALE:
THE TORTOISE MONSTER

Many cultures believe that tortoises are spiritual animals. This legend from Brazil tells how the Brazilian giant tortoise, once regarded as a monster that patrolled the path to the afterlife, became the gentle giant Brazilians know today.

One day long ago, a medicine man died. Like all people who died, the man had to cross the River of Death to reach the World of Eternal Souls. He looked over the steep bank at the wide, swiftly flowing river. He walked upriver for some distance and, seeing no bridge, walked back downriver again.

Finally, the man saw a bridge that led to a mound on the other side of the river. About halfway across the bridge, the man felt the bridge move beneath his feet. He looked down and saw that the bridge was the enormous tail of a tortoise that lay half buried in the mud on the other side of the river. The man ran quickly along the tortoise's tail, but before he could reach the other side of the river, the tortoise turned, opening its mouth to reveal glistening, sharp teeth, and raised its tail to toss the man into the river.

The man was instantly swept downstream by the rapid current, and his body was tossed against jagged rocks. Along the way, the man saw many of his kinsmen who had died before him, some on the riverbank unable to cross and some thrashing in the river as he was.

Fighting against the current, the man finally managed to climb back to shore. He knew that as long as the tortoise remained on the riverbank,

he and his kinsmen—as well as anyone who died after them—would be unable to cross the River of Death. The dead would not be able to reach the World of Eternal Souls with the tortoise preventing their passage.

The medicine man ran upstream to where the tortoise lay half buried in the mud. Using his magic, the man cast a spell to make an ax appear in his hand. Then he ran across the tortoise's tail as fast as he could. Just as the tortoise raised its tail to shake the man off, the man delivered a mighty blow with his ax, and the tortoise's tail fell into the river and was swept away.

The angry tortoise whirled around, exposing its sharp teeth. The man raised his ax again and chopped off the tortoise's head. Then he used the ax to fell a tree across the river, providing a safe bridge for all the dead who would need to cross into the World of Eternal Souls.

But the medicine man's satisfaction was short-lived, for he knew that all wild creatures act according to instinct, not malice. He forgave the tortoise for its behavior and searched for a way to revive it. He found a two-headed snake and cut off one of its heads. Then, using another spell, he joined it to the tortoise's body. He also healed the wound on the stump of the tortoise's tail.

The tortoise woke up and, discovering that it had no teeth, slowly crept away into the forest, never to return to the river. That is why, to this day, tortoises have stumpy tails and toothless mouths, and why they lead quiet lives in dry forests far from rivers.

GLOSSARY

aquatic – living or growing in water

captive-reared – raised in a place from which escape is not possible

commercial – used for business and to gain a profit rather than for personal reasons

deities – supreme beings, or gods and goddesses

ecotourists – people who travel to natural areas for the purpose of learning about conservation or ecology; they are typically guided by naturalists or other scientists

extinction – the act or process of becoming extinct: coming to an end or dying out

genetic – relating to genes, the basic physical units of heredity

herpetologists – people who study reptiles and their lives

hibernation – spending the winter in a sleeplike state in which breathing and heart rate slow down

Hindu – relating to Hinduism, the third-largest religion in the world

incubate – to keep an egg warm and protected until it is time for it to hatch

larvae – the newly hatched, wingless, often wormlike form of many insects before they become adults

metabolism – the processes that keep a body alive, including making use of food for energy

mummified – when a body has been preserved from decay by being filled and covered with plants, minerals, and oils

mythology – a collection of myths, or popular, traditional beliefs or stories that explain how something came to be or that are associated with a person or object

organic – obtained from living matter (such as plants or animals)

poaching – hunting protected species of wild animals, even though doing so is against the law

pupil – the dark, circular opening in the center of the eye through which light passes

seismic – relating to vibrations of the earth caused by tunneling, impacts, or earthquakes

solitary – alone, without companions

Tao – a philosophy, or system of thought, that originated in China in the sixth century B.C.

vertebrates – animals that have a backbone, including mammals, birds, reptiles, amphibians, and fish

webbed – connected by a web (of skin, as in the case of webbed feet)

SELECTED BIBLIOGRAPHY

Alderton, David. *Turtles & Tortoises of the World*. New York: Facts on File, 2003.

Branch, Bill. *Tortoises, Terrapins & Turtles of Africa*. Cape Town, South Africa: Struik Publishers, 2008.

Defenders of Wildlife. "Desert Tortoise." http://www .defenders.org/wildlife_and_habitat/wildlife/desert_ tortoise.php.

Gopher Tortoise Council. "About the Gopher Tortoise." http://www.gophertortoisecouncil.org/about.php.

Nichols, Henry. *Lonesome George: The Life and Loves of the World's Most Famous Tortoise*. London: Pan Macmillan, 2007.

Stanford, Craig B. *The Last Tortoise: A Tale of Extinction in Our Lifetime*. Cambridge: Belknap Press, 2010.

Left undisturbed, leopard tortoises of Africa's eastern and southern grasslands may live to be 100 years old.

INDEX